Praise for *Your Range Card for Life*

"As someone who has read project management books and books on leadership, military or civilian, *Your Range Card for Life* is a breath of fresh air. There are so many practical examples of how to plan and execute for success. Instead of motivational words and training stories, we get real world examples and paths for success. I really enjoyed John's analysis of creating a plan, some of which I already did without knowing why and much more to implement. Plus, it's full of wise insights into everyday life."

– John Hicks, Deputy Program Manager, DOE Contractor

"This book gives clear and practical structure to many of life's challenges that can cause us to feel overwhelmed, therefore putting off our goals or even giving up. I'm grateful John Riotte has taken the time to translate his military experience into these insightful techniques that anyone, in any position in life, can utilize. Unlike more idealized self-help books, we know these military techniques are tried and true under the most stressful and intense situations. Knowing John has successfully navigated such challenges helps me trust that these techniques can lead readers to their own personal success as well."

– Theresa M. Ward, Business Owner + Productivity Consultant

"As a collegiate head coach, I'm interacting with young adults who are faced with decisions, both important and trivial, on a daily basis. *Your Range Card for Life* is going to be my new "go-to" resource for strategies that I can help them implement to become the most successful, confident, and capable versions of themselves. The book is a practical, no-fluff guide for those in every stage of life."

– Darian Schmidt, Head Diving Coach, Southern Methodist University

"Explained in a manner that anyone can relate to and use to their advantage, John Riotte offers simple military techniques to help individuals identify an issue, determine key elements, develop multiple courses of action, and then preparing a logical plan to accomplish the objective. Take the two hours you need to read this book and apply what John is presenting here to address just one issue in your life. I bet you'll find the concepts in *Your Range Card for Life* will become tools you can use over and over again. If you're an educator, I challenge you to use this training aid to assist your students in developing their analytical skills. Semper Fi!"

– Pat McGilton, Retired Marine

"*Your Range Card for Life* is the civilian 'SparkNotes™' of the internal voice and subconscious reasoning I imagine the child of a military vet would have. While we're not all lucky enough to have these decision-making skills and strategies ingrained in us from a wise parent, the concepts are logical and simple to adapt. Our lives are more hectic, busy, and anxiety-ridden than ever before, but with these strategies, we can all take a clearer look at what we aim to achieve and have the toolbox to make it happen."

– Alexandra Schmidt

Your Range Card for Life

Military Management Techniques to Help Control the Everyday Chaos

by John Riotte

Published by How2Conquer
Atlanta, GA
www.how2conquer.com

© 2022 by John Riotte

All rights reserved. This book or any portion thereof may not be reproduced or used in any manner whatsoever without the express written permission of the author except for the use of brief quotations in a book review.

First edition, August 2022

Illustrations and cover design by Telia Garner
Edited by Emily M. Owens

Library of Congress Control Number: 2022943091

Print ISBN 978-1-945783-18-0
Ebook ISBN 978-1-945783-19-7

For information about special discounts available for bulk purchases, please contact How2Conquer Special Sales at www.how2conquer.com/bulk-orders.

This book is dedicated to my family and friends. I am so blessed to have you all in my life.

I also want to thank the lovely people who believed in me when I doubted myself, and those who saw something in me when I could not see anything ahead of me.

Thank you all!

JJR

Contents

My Hope for You 1
How to Use This Book 4
    The Techniques Buffet 4
    Four Essential Tips 5
    In Your Toolkit: Confidence 7
Visualizing Your Position: The Range Card (RC) 9
    What's a Range Card? 9
    Developing Your Range Card 11
    Validating a Range Card 14
    Review and Reflection 15
    Range Card Example: Getting a Promotion 17
Focusing Amid Distraction: Peripheral Vision
Competition-Evaluation (PVC-E) 22
    What's a Peripheral Vision Competition-Evaluation? 22
    How Did the PVC-E Come About? 23
    How to Complete a PVC-E 24
    PVC-E Example: Not Getting That Promotion 27
Developing Situational Awareness: Observe, Orient,
Decide, Act (OODA) Loop 30
    What's an OODA Loop? 30
    Completing an OODA Loop 31
    OODA Example: The Weekend Barbecue 33

Plotting the Path Forward: Observation, Cover, Obstacles,
Key Terrain, Avenues of Approach (OCOKA) 35

    What's OCOKA? 35

    Analyzing OCOKA 36

    OCOKA Example: Being Intentional in Your Career 44

Getting from A to B: Primary, Alternate, Contingency,
Emergency (PACE) Planning 48

    What's PACE Planning? 48

    Primary, Alternate, Contingency, and Emergency Plans 49

    Reflection in PACE Planning 51

    PACE Planning Example: Revisiting Promotion and
    Progression 53

Chaos Management: Mission, Equipment, Troops, Time
Available (METT) - Terrain, Civilians, Politics (TCP) 57

    What's METT-TCP? 57

    Conducting a METT-TCP Assessment 64

    METT-TCP Example: The VIP Tour 66

Clarifying the Operation: Tasks, Conditions, and
Standards 69

    What are Tasks, Conditions, and Standards? 69

    The Right to Clarity 72

    Tasks, Conditions, and Standards Example: Parking
    for the VIP Tour 73

Your Turn 76

    Breaking Down These Techniques 76

    What If These Techniques Don't Work? 79

Contents

Conclusion 83

Resources 84

    Suggested Reading 84

    Glossary 84

Acknowledgements 88

About the Author 90

My Hope for You

When I decided to write this book, I was spending an afternoon puttering around my garage like many older men like to do. I looked up, and the Sandia Mountains surrounding my home in Albuquerque were particularly beautiful. I'm not the first guy to find himself in a philosophical mood when presented with a beautiful view, but something about the mountains that day made me do some deep thinking about my life – where I am, how I got here, and how the things I've learned along the way could help someone else.

I find myself doing what all lucky people get to do: getting older. The bad parts of this experience are pretty well-defined by the media (and the creaky knees of anyone who has had a life full of action and activity), but the good part is being able to see where my choices have led to good outcomes. Of course, I can also see how *not* following the advice I'll give you in this book led to less-than-stellar moments in my life. I'm the example both of why the program I'm going to lay out works and what happens when you don't follow my advice.

I've always been a goal-driven guy. I want to win. Tell me how to win, and I'm all in. It's what made the military a perfect career for an intense young man like I was.

I was nineteen years old when I joined the United States Army, and I had the pleasure and privilege of serving my country for twenty years. I loved it. I got to live a seven-year-old kid's dream – *I got to be GI Joe*. I jumped out of planes (please see above note about my knees), ran through the woods, and was surrounded by a group of warriors who – in the eyes of a young 19-year-old – seemed to accomplish the impossible, often with minimal resources, little guidance, and a tight timeline.

As I moved through the ranks from taking orders to giving orders (and becoming responsible for the outcome), I learned and applied the same techniques I'll share with you here.

I separated from the military in October 2000. I use the word "separated" because "retired" never felt right. It would be like telling a doctor they're no longer a doctor just because they're no longer employed by a hospital – it just doesn't work. The Army shaped my adult life; it's an essential part of who I am. With the guidance of some of the finest officers and NCOs[1] from every background imaginable, I learned valuable life lessons.

I learned that effort is good, but results are what people see. Results are used to measure us against others for promotions, raises, and bonuses; they affect how we are viewed by others. Results also inform how we rate ourselves against our own standards in life, how we judge our personal successes and efforts.

Most importantly, I learned that if I was going to have any results against which to measure my success, I needed to have a plan. Great things don't happen if there's no planning process – they can't happen, because often things just don't get done if there's no roadmap to guide the way.

I've lived a great life, and I've met my goals using what I learned as a 19-year-old kid. Perhaps the greatest thing about getting older is that you want to help other people succeed, and you have a lot of knowledge to help them do it. Not everyone has the benefit of military service to shape their character and teach them the framework and foresight necessary to thoroughly plan and *fully* achieve their goals.

In this book, you'll encounter terms that are repeated and reinforced again and again. Repetition will help you train

---

[1] Non-commissioned officers usually earn positions of authority by promotion through the enlisted ranks. A commissioned officer is an officer who has rank before officially assuming their role, usually because they enter the military after receiving a post-secondary degree.

yourself to automatically begin your chosen planning process, and you'll find that you see things and evaluate situations more quickly and with more clarity. It can happen, and it will happen.

So, enjoy your journey. You'll have successes, and you'll have some failures, but you'll learn from both.

Be good to yourself. You're worth it.

John

How to Use This Book

All the techniques and methods you'll read here can work for you. When I use them, I don't feel as if so many things in my life are spinning out of control – I feel better able to manage my chaos. I feel empowered and like I have a better handle on things, which allows me – and will allow you – to move through the day with confidence. How? Because you'll have a plan to manage your days; and by managing your days, you can begin the process of moving toward your future goals.

The techniques in this book all interact and intertwine; they'll reference, complement, and refer to each other. There are common themes in each method I'll present to you, so we'll take a look back at them in the section "Breaking Down these Techniques" at the end.

Remember: There's never a one-size-fits-all approach to life, so there cannot be a one-size-fits-all approach to how you manage your life.

The Techniques Buffet

I like to think about these techniques like a buffet. You can pick one, pick two, or even mix a few of the options. Serve yourself – choose what works and discard what doesn't.

I hope you find something that makes a difference for you and how you approach decision making and planning. All the techniques we'll discuss can be modified to your needs. Don't worry if you find something doesn't work for you the way you thought it would – it happens. Go back and try something else, or better yet – modify based on what you've discovered and make it work for you! Thorough planning has been the bedrock of my success in life, but flexibility is just as key.

A great plan accounts for the unexpected and reflects our ability to react, modify, and adapt.

Four Essential Tips

1. You need to have a plan. Nothing in life succeeds without a good plan.

You may have a quick, short-term success, but to be competitive and achieve your goals reliably – you need to be able to break bigger goals down into achievable pieces. Tasks become steps, then steps become actions to be taken.

Planning is the easy part, and it's an excellent way to find out who you are – you consider your likes, dislikes, strengths, weaknesses, values, fears, and convictions. Without knowing who you are, you can't know where you want to go.

Look at the successful people around you: colleagues or leaders you admire, a winning athlete on your favorite team, a musician whose work you enjoy. It's a well-worn adage worth repeating: People aren't handed success. Successful people make a series of smaller life plans supporting big goals. They didn't just "go for it" and hope for the best. They made a plan, set goals and target points, adjusted and revised, and learned from mistakes and failures along the way. Did they all fail at some point? You bet! But they held onto their passion and belief in themselves. They had a vision of success and a plan to achieve it.

Remember – life happens in seconds, then in minutes and hours, days and years. Small actions can build up to achieve those big, seemingly impossible goals.

If we need a plan, then we need to have a planning process. That's where this book comes in – techniques for planning and managing your goals in life. Everyone's plan is unique, so don't worry if yours seems different.

2. You need a team.

Behind every successful person is an effective team. The challenge is creating that team and providing them with the guidance, resources, and leadership to succeed.

No one can do it all on their own. You can be the greatest football coach ever, but without a game plan, a star quarterback, a great offensive line, a solid receiving corps, and a strong defense – you will not win. A great CEO cannot be great without a hired team of top performers who know what needs to be done and have the resources necessary to do it.

You may not have a staff or a wide receiver, but the people in your life like your spouse, parents, friends – even your kids and maybe your boss – can all form a supportive team to help keep your plans on track.

3. You must *communicate* the plan!

What good is a plan if no one knows how good it is? Once you've identified your team, you have to make them aware of your plan, the steps it'll take to complete, and where they fit into the equation.

Like I'm sure you have, I've been roped into bad plans before – poorly conceived, unreviewed, and inadequately resourced. It's no surprise when these plans fail, but poor communication can sink even great plans (and relationships). Start communicating at the beginning and continue throughout the planning process, making sure everyone involved is on the same page and has the opportunity to contribute. This also helps ensure your team will be more invested in the plan, and some might even have their own advice to share. A good plan requires good leadership, but the more minds involved in the preliminary stages, the more likely you'll be able to catch snags before they become big obstacles.

4. Don't be afraid of self-evaluation or failure.

Many people run from self-reflection, especially when it comes to failure. Thinking about what you've done wrong or messed up is scary, but you just need to change your perspective. If self-evaluation is only a chance to fixate on your weaknesses and berate yourself, you won't learn.

Honest self-evaluation allows us to grow; it's an opportunity to be and do better. So instead of focusing on the failure itself, be honest about what worked and what didn't. Use it as an opportunity to highlight for yourself how you've improved and how you'll be more prepared and experienced next time.

We may separate our greatest successes and failures when we reflect on our lives, but we can always learn from both. Without failure, we wouldn't have learned many important life lessons. Evaluation is an important part of the planning process, and many excellent plans have been inspired by failure. Reflecting on those failures can help you take greater control of where you want to go.

In Your Toolkit: Confidence

Confidence is one of the most important tools we'll need for a successful journey. It's always been inside us, and we can see it in others, but sometimes we need to remind ourselves it's there. Believing in your ability to accomplish something is important, but remember that confidence comes in other forms too. Trust in your ability to commit to your plan, learn from mistakes, continue improving, and (most importantly) take that first step towards a goal.

STANDARD RANGE CARD

MAGNETIC NORTH	Brief description of the goal you intend to accomplish with this range card

DATA SECTION

DTG			
OBJECT	DESCRIPTION	OBJECT	DESCRIPTION

A Range Card creates a visual representation of where you are, where you want to go, and how you'll get there.

Visualizing Your Position: The Range Card (RC)

Primary Goal/Usage: Use a Range Card to evaluate situations, remain true to yourself and your values, and plan next steps by visualizing where you are.

Time to Complete: 10-15 minutes

The Range Card is one of my favorite techniques. In fact, I use it on an almost daily basis. It's a great method of planning because it allows you to quickly and effectively visualize your surroundings and where you want to go.

What's a Range Card?

A Range Card helps you create a picture of your situation. It allows you to see what lies between you and a goal – whether it's obstacles, potential dangers, resources, or milestones to check your progress. It includes what you know, what you don't yet know, and charts a clear path to success.

Key Terms

- **Date Time Group (DTG)** is the date and time a Range Card is made. The military has a standard format, but you can note it however you choose. The DTG indicates when a Range Card was made, and it helps you index them by date as you revise and update the plan.
- **Dead Space** includes areas you cannot easily see but know something is there. It could represent unforeseen issues, roadblocks, things to be prepared for that could go wrong, or even invisible opportunities. Dead space is the object in your path most likely to change over time because as you learn new information, you'll become aware of new uncertainties and questions.
- **Known Distance Markers** are objects ahead that you already know the distance to from your current position. They could be milestones, deadlines, or progress markers.
- **Obstacles** could be known issues, roadblocks, or weaknesses you can observe in a specific area between you and the goal.
- **Target Reference Points (TRP)** are easily recognizable, always visible locations (natural or manmade) used for target acquisition and to determine range. These could be days you set on the calendar to check if you're on track.
- **Left and Right Limits** are the imaginary lines identifying your area of responsibility, stretching from your location to a designated point. Depending on when you create a Range Card, this area could widen or shrink. Your Left and Right Limits help keep you from straying from your path; they can control distractions and allow you to focus on what's in front of you.
- The **Final Protective Line (FPL)** is the farthest you can go before straying into another person's area or betraying one of your own personal boundaries. Crossing that line could mean encroaching on someone else's space (physical or otherwise) or compromising your values.

Developing Your Range Card

To develop your Range Card, you need to first orient yourself to your surroundings – what's ahead of you as well as any limits to your left and right.

Where is Your Magnetic North?

Magnetic North is the point you're focused on; it's what's leading you forward and providing direction. To find your Magnetic North, ask yourself: Where is my goal? What am I facing or working towards? This goal can be personal or professional, short- or long-term – anything you consider a goal.

Your Magnetic North also reflects who you are and how you wish to see yourself – your sense of identity, values, standards of conduct, boundaries, and what you hold close. It's what pushes you to move in a certain direction through your environment – both your path and the way you will follow this path. If you don't know where north is or what's driving you towards it, your planning process will be flawed, and you may fail to achieve your goals.

What's in Front of You?

What do you see? What will you have to avoid, work around, or embrace on your journey? Not everything is an obstacle that could cause harm or be a hindrance; some things may also help, even if just to provide protection or support and comfort. No matter what you see ahead, you need know what's there so you can anticipate and perhaps prepare for it. Over time and with experience, you'll get better at defining what you see and determining if it's a threat or an asset.

Imagine the metaphorical space between where you are and where you want to be. Start making a list of things you might encounter. You're just starting to do some thinking and planning, so they don't have to be specifically positive or negative at this point.

They might include:

- **Known Distance Markers**
    - Calendar-based markers, like deadlines or upcoming events
    - Task- or deliverable-based markers, like completing a small piece of a larger project
- **Obstacles**
    - Common issues others may have faced while working toward a similar goal, or ones you've faced before
    - Areas you know you need to improve or progress in by learning or practicing something
- **Opportunities**
    - Strengths you can use to your advantage
    - Events or programs you could sign up for
- **Holistic Considerations**
    - Potential impacts on other areas of your life, such as work, financial, health, family, personal, etc.
- **Resources**
    - Learning and practice opportunities
    - Books, articles, or other forms of instruction and guidance
    - Colleagues or mentors who might be able to help or provide guidance

Review your list – before adding an item to your Range Card, consider how it might affect you. Is it something positive or could it cause drama, negative energy, confusion, or chaos for you? You might not know just yet. Sometimes you can't be sure if something is positive or negative until other things pan out, and that's okay.

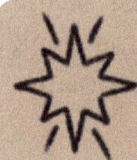 All obstacles can become opportunities for us to achieve our goals.

Dead Space: How Can You Anticipate What You Can't See?

For its typical use on a Range Card, dead space seems like a pretty simple concept. If something's blocking your view – such as hills, buildings, or another natural or man-made terrain feature – it's easy to notice just by looking up. But how do you anticipate metaphorical "dead space"?

Someone I used to know liked to say, when learning something new, "I don't know what I don't know." You might have heard the phrase before, but it means feeling so out of your depth you don't even know what questions to ask. Everyone has been in that situation before, so don't be afraid to admit to feeling a little lost – there might be someone who can share some advice or a little of their own experience as guidance, or even someone who knows the terrain of what started as dead space for you.

On your Range Card, dead space can take many forms. To be considered for a promotion, maybe you know you need to ace an upcoming presentation, but your last one didn't go so well because an important source dropped out at the last minute. You didn't see it coming then, but this time, you could have a list of backup experts to interview. Or maybe you don't know who else is up for the same promotion and what they're doing to get it. Potential technical issues could be the last area of dead space in your path. Just in case, you have the presentation saved in the cloud, on a USB drive, in your email, and a few printed copies on hand.

On the battlefield, the Range Card is a literal record of your surroundings, but creating a Range Card for goals is more abstract than moving physically from point A to point B – it takes a bit of imagination. But it also takes imagination to come up with creative solutions to problems you'll face on the way to achieving your goals!

The Range Card is intended to be a living document, so the next time you pause to update or redraw it from a new position, you'll know more – that dead space might be smaller, you may have a new plan for managing it, or maybe you'll have new friends or family as sources of insight to propel you forward on your path.

What Are Your LRLs (Left and Right Limits)?

Who's on your left and right? How do you fit into their areas of responsibility? How far can you go before you step into someone else's area? How do they tie into yours? How do you cover them, and how do they cover you? How can you support each other? How will you respect their space and how will they respect yours?

Whatever area of your life is the focus of your goal – personal, professional, etc. – will determine who is to your left and right, but your relationship with them will affect how you fit together. For example, some family members may not be part of your usual support network, but if you're planning a reunion together, you'll still need to figure out how to work best with Aunt Marguerite.

Your Final Protective Line will help you establish the Left and Right Limits. It's often easy to tell when you've crossed that line. If Aunt Marguerite always makes the chicken salad, you'll probably feel guilty if you bring your own version, too.

Don't encroach on Aunt Marguerite's chicken salad. Define your Left and Right Limits ahead of time, so your area of responsibility is clear.

Validating a Range Card

Once a Range Card is complete, you need someone to look over it to review what you've seen and understood. Isn't it always better to bounce an idea off someone else to see if it makes sense? Having another person validate your Range Card allows you to gain more clarity and identify areas you might need to improve the next time around.

Validating a Range Card can go deeper than just checking if it seems right. Depending on how personal your goal is, it could be a difficult process and, to a degree, a moment where you have to open yourself up to another person. Part of your growth is in trusting others. Remember the Left and Right Limits, your support? This is where you'll call on that support network – trusted friends, colleagues, or family members – to help you make an honest assessment of where you are and where you want to be.

Review and Reflection

A Range Card is just a snapshot in time. It tells you where you were at a specific point, but it will be outdated eventually – so it's important to look for opportunities to reevaluate.

An important part of using a Range Card is reflection. You need to continually consider where you've been and where you want to go. It's good to set a regular time to do this review, like during your morning commute, in the shower, or when you're getting ready to start your day. Anytime is a good time to pause, reflect, assess, and review. When you feel your position has changed significantly, you may even want to set aside some time to reflect on your progress and redraw your Range Card. (That's why you marked it with a DTG!) Keeping up-to-date versions of your Range Card is not only useful for recording new information as you progress along your path – it's also a great opportunity to reflect on and be inspired by your successes.

Each time you look back, you can ask yourself if you were as accurate or aware as you thought when you developed that Range Card, and you can improve your ability to refine it even more. Over time, this ongoing review process will become more natural and help you enhance your skills.

You can learn so much from yourself if you just take a moment to reflect. If you're not afraid to change, you can grow and become more mindful and adaptable. Everyone can change, and most likely will, so why not take control of your trajectory?

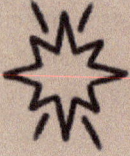 A good NCO will tell you, "If you're not constantly evaluating your situation, you're doing it wrong!"

Range Card Example: Getting a Promotion

Let's look at an example. Joanne has been working for the same company for a few years now, and she wants to work toward getting a promotion. Joanne has been inspired by leaders who supported her in the past and wants to pay it forward, but she knows she needs more leadership experience.

We'll start with questions Joanne might ask herself to determine a plan with steps to take and actions to accomplish. Some items may be recorded in more than one area. Then we'll explore what this would look like on Joanne's Range Card.

Questions and Considerations

» Is a position within my area open or will a new role be opening soon? Why is the position available? If it's a new position, is the role fully defined yet? If it's an existing role, why did the last person leave? Did they quit, get promoted, reassigned, or let go – and why? These items could be dead space, since I might not know yet.

» Am I qualified for this promotion? Do I meet the required and/or desired criteria for this position? Higher levels of management have determined the skills, level of experience, certifications, and background an employee needs to be successful in the position. I need to be honest with myself: If the position requires an advanced degree or certification I don't have, I might not be considered for it. Identifying required versus desired criteria can be an obstacle.

» Once I've identified an obstacle – like a required certification – I can begin to look for ways to go over, around, or through it. How do I get certified, and what dates/deadlines should I set to check my progress (Target Reference Points)? How long will it take to get this certification? How much will it cost? Can I balance my job and working toward this requirement? Will this certification improve my skill set and help me find a better place in my field?

» Who should I talk to about this position (family, friends, co-workers)? My support team can help me understand my areas of responsibility (Left and Right Limits) and what is in front of me as I prepare for this journey. I can ask them questions like: Do you think this is a good fit for me? What does this promotion really mean (more money, hours, and responsibility)?

 Remember, your support team can assist you and give you a level of clarity you might not have on your own.

Joanne's Range Card Notes	
Goal/Objective: What's My Magnetic North?	
My goal is to be promoted within my organization. I have an opportunity to apply for a newly created role managing two other colleagues. I know we are planning to hire more staff in my current position, and I've been inspired by past managers who helped me adjust as a new employee and continue progressing during my time here. I believe I have knowledge to share, and I'd love to support our team, but I know I need more coaching experience.	
Observation: What's in Front of Me?	
Date Time Group (DTG)	March 10, 2022

Joanne's Range Card Notes

Known Distance Markers	I setup a 1:1 meeting with my manager next week to discuss my professional development. I'll be helping our new interns get started the following week. Interviews for new hires will begin in two months.
Target Reference Points (TRP)	With my manager's help, I'll have a learning/development plan in place the Friday before our interns start. After our two-week onboarding process, I'll gather feedback from our interns to discover any gaps or opportunities and present to my manager. I'm enrolled in an online leadership and coaching certification course that ends one month before interviews begin.
Dead Space	My workload has been a little lighter than usual recently, but if we get more client projects this month, I know I may need to prioritize some deadlines over coaching/learning opportunities – which could throw a wrench in my progression plan.
Obstacles	I've only led interns once before, so I need to strengthen my leadership knowledge/experience. My coaching course runs every Wednesday from 6-7pm, so I'll need to block out my schedule to make sure I'm not double-booked.

Joanne's Range Card Notes	
Opportunities	I've held leadership positions in volunteer activities before, and I learned a lot from the experience. I've signed up for a professional development networking group, and sometimes they offer one-day courses and events.
Resources	My manager and my colleague, Barbara, will both be invaluable resources. They've already recommended three books on coaching and leadership.
Holistic considerations: What Are My Left and Right Limits?	
Left/Right Limits	My colleague, Barbara, will also be supporting our interns during onboarding, so we've discussed individual responsibilities. We have an optional 15-minute meeting set for the end of each onboarding session to review how it's going, so if anything changes or if other priorities come up, we can assist each other.
Final Protective Line (FPL)	Barbara has a lot of experience with interns, and she knows I'd love any feedback or advice she has after seeing me work. I know she has to leave by 4:30pm each day to pick up her child, so if an intern needs to meet or stay later, I have agreed to do so.

Visualizing Your Position: The Range Card

Joanne's Range Card

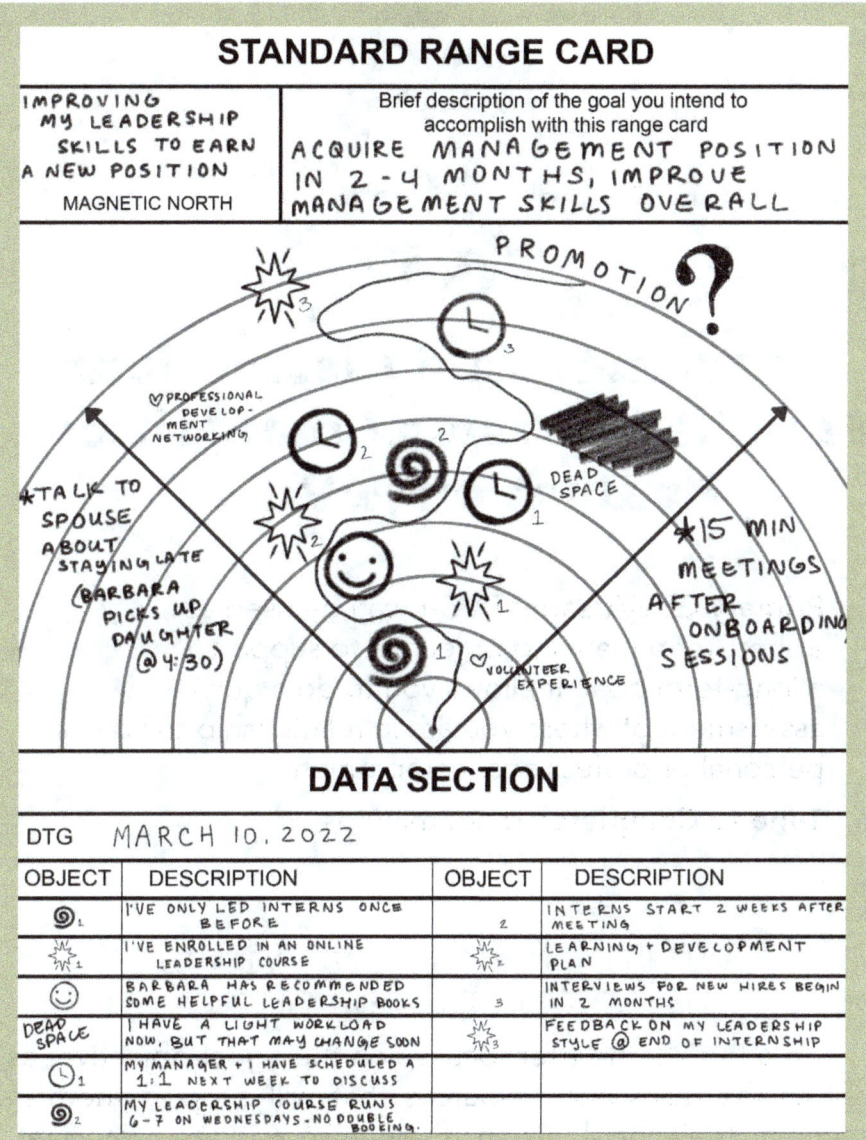

Focusing Amid Distraction: Peripheral Vision Competition-Evaluation (PVC-E)

Primary Goal/Usage: PVC-E can be used as a short-term planning objective to support a long-term goal. It allows you to do a quick assessment of where you are in relationship to your personal or professional competition.

Time to Complete: 15-20 minutes

What's a Peripheral Vision Competition-Evaluation?

In a PVC-E, the user focuses on their goal/objective, as well as the tasks and resources that will support them in reaching their goal. Then they acknowledge, interpret, project, and plan for the opportunities, threats, and evaluations that could occur along the way. If you've ever completed a SWOT analysis before (a strategic planning technique used to review Strengths, Weaknesses, Opportunities, and Threats related to business or project planning), the PVC-E takes a similar approach.

> ## Key Terms
>
> » **Peripheral Vision** Like Left/Right Limits used in the Range Card, **Peripheral Vision** looks at what is around you and how you tie into the person/position on your left and right.
> » **Competition** is anything that could be competing for your time or focus while pursuing a goal.
> » **Evaluation** is an honest review that considers a set of tasks against predefined measures of success and determines if these measures were achieved.

How Did the PVC-E Come About?

Many years ago, I was watching three accomplished marksmen go through a drill with pump shotguns. They were instructed to load, aim, and shoot at a target. There was no time constraint to the exercise; the goal was just to focus on weapon manipulation and body mechanic skills. But all three were making some basic mistakes, mistakes they should not have made. I knew something was wrong but wasn't sure what.

I stopped the drill, re-explained the objectives of the exercise, and we started again. Again, these three began making the same mistakes. I couldn't figure out what was going on.

I had to look at the *reasons* for the mistakes rather than the mistakes themselves. Why would an accomplished marksman make a basic mistake and not realize why?

The answer was so simple.

Instead of focusing on body mechanics and successfully engaging a target, they were using their peripheral vision to see what the other soldiers were doing. In watching someone else, they lost sight of the objective of the drill and forgot their own goals.

So, what did I do to assist them?

I had them stop and do the drill by themselves, one at a time. You may have heard the saying, "slow is smooth, smooth is fast" – and that's just what I told them. They did very well going one at a time, then two at a time, then all together.

How you remain focused on your goals, and to what degree of success you achieve them, is what PVC-E is about. Competition will always be at work in and around your path to your goals, but the PVC-E is about taking stock of what or who could be competing for your attention and prioritizing the demands in your life effectively.

How to Complete a PVC-E

Peripheral Vision

PVC-E looks at how you and your goals relate to people and circumstances around you, so the first step is to ask questions about your periphery. In daily life, this might be the people you rely on most, like close friends, family, or team members you often collaborate with at work. You may need to rely on them for support, as they may need to rely on you. They need to know what you see, and you need to know what they see. Circumstances could include existing commitments and goals – anything that may require your attention.

Ask yourself some of the following questions:

- » Where am I in relation to my current environment?
- » What is happening around me?
- » What events can or will affect my current environment?
- » How do outside forces and events influence the relationship between me, my environment, and my goals?

When you begin to analyze your PVC-E by putting your thoughts on paper, you actually start to develop the beginnings of a Range Card.

Competition

In our professional and personal lives, we have goals we set and goals that are set for us by others, but there will always be other things going on along the sidelines. You need to maintain focus to avoid losing sight of what's really important – the objective.

Take the marksmen I mentioned earlier. They each had the same goal, but the simple act of comparing themselves to others distracted them from it. They may have felt like they were competing against each other, but really that contest was competing for their attention and distracting them from their true goal.

Always be aware of your surroundings but focus on what you're working to achieve.

Evaluation

A PVC-E allows you to consider your goal, what you need to accomplish that goal, what level of support you may need, and how you'll determine success. How many times have you been told to do something but weren't given all the information? Don't you want to know what you're supposed to be doing? Evaluating yourself will help you identify gaps in the future. The next time you review your progress, you'll probably want to consider if the metrics you're using are really helping you.

When you conduct the evaluation portion of a PVC-E, you must be honest. If you can't be honest with yourself, how can you be honest with others?

Note that I said *honest*, not mean. Sometimes people confuse an honest evaluation with mean-spirited "feedback," where someone is ripped into, called names, and then shown the door. Nothing could be further from the truth, and taking a "celebrity roast" approach to evaluation doesn't help anyone. Fair evaluations must be conducted without bias, prejudice, or animosity.

Does that mean you can gloss over things that didn't quite go right? Of course not! No one wants to think they're doing a good job only to get the rug pulled out when someone tells them the truth. Being honest – even when it's difficult – is more constructive than sugarcoating ever will be, and whether you're evaluating yourself or someone else, it opens opportunities to improve, learn, and develop new skills.

Conducting an evaluation is about learning, not tearing someone down. It's about taking a closer look at something and determining what's working, what could be better, and collaborating on possible improvements.

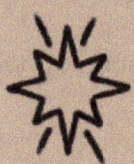

An honest evaluation is just what it says – honest. An evaluation takes a set of tasks, placed against a measure of success, and then determines if the measures of success were achieved.

PVC-E Example: Not Getting That Promotion

What if Joanne didn't get that promotion from the Range Card example? Everyone has failed at something before, even things that felt like the perfect fit. But what's more important than the failure itself is how you respond to it. After you mourn what didn't work out, what will you do next? Try again? Aim for a new goal?

Failure sucks, but it's necessary to get to the good stuff. You've probably heard the saying about how if you never try, you'll never fail. I prefer Samuel Beckett's take: "Ever tried. Ever failed. No matter. Try Again. Fail again. Fail better."

Questions and Considerations

Before starting her PVC-E, Joanne might consider the following.

- » Think about peers in my field. Are they getting promoted, and if so, why? I've always been told to look at success. Try what's helping someone else be successful.
- » Conversely, look at what my less successful peers are doing and *don't* do those things. Learning from other's failed efforts, I can ask myself, "Why didn't that work? What could I do differently?"
- » Evaluate what went wrong. Were there inadequate resources, financial issues, lack of direction/guidance, lack of commitment to the goal, scheduling issues, or something else? (Note that these are reasons something didn't work, not excuses. Reasons should be factually based, verifiable, and realistically improvable.)

Joanne's PVC-E

Observation and Holistic Considerations: Peripheral Vision

I didn't get the promotion, but the feedback I got from the hiring team was constructive. They chose another colleague for the role, Mary, who has been with the company about 2-3 years longer than I have. My manager is continuing to support and encourage my development, and Barbara has been a great mentor.

I knew I needed more coaching experience, but there's nothing I can do about experience in terms of time. What I can do is focus on my learning/development plan, continue to support the intern program, and find other ways to contribute and develop my leadership skills.

Opportunities and Threats: Competition

Mary already leads another group of interns, but I know I'm not in competition with her. We set up a time next week to chat about courses and resources she's found helpful, and I've made myself available if she ever needs a hand training her new team.

Before my interview, I had to miss a few of the classes for my coaching course because I decided to work late instead. One of the last ones was an especially important lesson, and I regretted missing it. When my manager heard, he offered to be an accountability buddy.

Joanne's PVC-E

Evaluation

Aside from needing more experience, what I think really went wrong was the interview itself. I got really nervous and fumbled through the first questions, even though I was feeling more confident by the end. I'd learned a lot over the past two months, but it's been a while since I did an interview, and I should have practiced more in preparation.

One reason I didn't practice enough was that the week before the interview, we received a lot more client work, and I needed to pitch in on projects I don't usually work on. The next time I have an interview, I will block out time in my schedule for interview prep and hold myself accountable.

Developing Situational Awareness: Observe, Orient, Decide, Act (OODA) Loop

Primary Goal/Usage: OODA is a quick snapshot of a planning process. If you've made a plan using the OODA Loop, you can always revise and go deeper with another technique later.

Time to Complete: 10-15 minutes

What's an OODA Loop?

In the military, the OODA Loop is a method of quick decision making intended to help you leverage your agility over an opponent's brute force advantage in combat. The idea is that under pressure, good decisions are made in rapid succession on a loop of Observing, Orienting, Deciding, and Acting. If you can train yourself to work through the OODA Loop quickly, you can use your levelheadedness against an attack and interrupt your opponent's less refined reaction cycle.

Hopefully, if combat is one of the challenges you face in everyday life, someone has already mentioned this one to you – but in the likely event that it's not, the OODA Loop can

> ## Key Terms
>
> » **Observing** is taking a snapshot of your surroundings and the situation at hand.
> » **Orienting** is about adjusting your focus and resources towards what needs to be done.
> » **Decisions** are made quickly to determine a course of action (CoA).
> » A **Course of Action (CoA)** is the immediate next steps you've chosen. It should be feasible and complete.
> » **Acting** happens when you set your CoA in motion.

easily be used to make quick and effective decisions to accomplish small goals, anticipate crises, and put out those "fires" that crop up in your daily life. Let's talk about what makes up the OODA Loop and how you can use it to boost your decision-making skills and efficiency.

Completing an OODA Loop

Observe

Much like when creating a Range Card, you have to observe your surroundings. What happened, what's happening now, and what's most likely going to happen? Sometimes when presented with an unexpected challenge, our minds shut down – surprise or shock can make it difficult to make informed decisions in the moment, but with practice, you can build resilience and become better at working through this initial distress.

To react effectively, you'll have to take an honest account of what's going on. You'll also need to do so quickly – the OODA Loop is about reacting efficiently to a challenge that's appeared in your path.

Orient

After you've observed what's happened, you can begin the planning process and orient your actions and resources toward what you want or need to do.

Decide

After you've observed what's happening, oriented your resources, and conducted a good planning process, you must decide upon a Course of Action (CoA).

Act

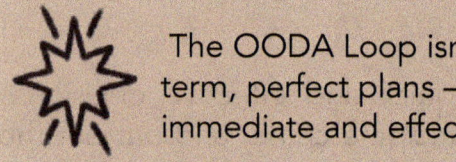

The OODA Loop isn't intended for long term, perfect plans – it's for taking immediate and effective action.

Once you've decided your CoA, you must act. But have you ever noticed that sometimes action is the hardest part of a planning process?

We've all found ourselves in situations before where we feel nervous and apprehensive about the future. Don't worry, that's normal. Just remember that on every journey, everything starts with a first step. What is it you're usually afraid of – failure or embarrassment at not achieving goals? We all fail sometimes, but failure is just an opportunity to learn.

Whether or not you make the right choice under pressure is a matter of practice and luck, but it's essential that you act!

OODA Example: The Weekend Barbecue

You probably use some components of the OODA Loop every day, just under lower stakes than immediate physical danger. Let's look at an example, this time with Joanne's friend, Ralph. We'll skip the Questions and Considerations section though, since the OODA Loop is intended to be used for effective, in-the-moment planning and response.

Ralph is hosting a weekend barbecue for friends and family. Everything is going well, the food is delicious, and his guests are having a lovely time. Then, the unthinkable happens – Ralph feels a raindrop. Luckily he remembers a planning technique Joanne introduced him to last week, and he starts his first OODA Loop.

Ralph's OODA Loop

Observe

First, simply observe what's already happened and what's about to happen. How hard is it raining? What's at risk of being rained on? Maybe rain will just dampen the mood, or maybe there's food out that would be ruined by moisture. The faster I figure out or accept what's happening (read: the less time spent playing "was that a raindrop?"), the faster and more effectively I can work through the loop.

Orient

Where are we and what are my options? Since we're in my backyard, can I put up a shelter quickly enough to mitigate the rain's impact? Can everyone scurry into the house and keep having a nice time? What else will I need to do after a location change – find more chairs, help guests dry off, clear off surfaces to house displaced hot dogs?

Ralph's OODA Loop

Decide

Since I'm hosting the barbecue at home, I had the forethought to acquire a pop-up tent in case of rain. It'll only take a few minutes to set up, but it's raining hard enough that the hamburger buns will be soggy by then. I have a covered back porch, so I can mobilize a group of my guests to temporarily transport the food to shelter while another group helps me quickly set up the tent and dry off tables and chairs.

Act

I split my guests into groups and quickly give them clear instructions to help execute the plan. I locate, gather, and stage all the necessary equipment (towels, tent, helpers), and we set up the tent right away. With just a few moments of clear-headed decision making (and help from my impromptu team), the barbecue is saved!

Plotting the Path Forward: Observation, Cover, Obstacles, Key Terrain, Avenues of Approach (OCOKA)

Primary Goal/Usage: OCOKA allows you to plot a path forward by looking at routes and terrain, obstacles and how to address them, as well as areas of advantage.

Time to Complete: 20 minutes

What's OCOKA?

OCOKA stands for Observation and Fields of Fire, Cover and Concealment, Obstacles (manmade and natural), Key Terrain, and Avenues of Approach. You'll notice that we've seen some of these terms before, so they'll become more familiar as you use these techniques over time.

Key Terms

» A **Primary Route** is the route which will best support your movement toward an objective.
» An **Alternative Route** is similar to the Primary Route and still a good option, but it might have more obstacles or take longer.
» A **Contingency Route** will get you there, but it's the least desirable path.
» **Observation** involves taking in your surroundings and being situationally aware, allowing you to plot a path forward.
» **Cover** provides protection and hides you from the enemy.
» **Concealment** allows you to observe what's happening around you while obscuring your position.
» **Obstacles** are issues, roadblocks, or weaknesses you can observe in a specific area.
» **Key Terrain** are areas that could give an advantage.
» **Avenues of Approach** are how you move along a chosen route based on the terrain. How do you approach a problem or an opportunity?

Analyzing OCOKA

Observation

This term keeps popping up, doesn't it? Observation is all about taking in your surroundings – where you've been, where you are, and where you want to be. In the military, we call this situational awareness, and it contributes to your ability to plot a path forward.

You need to:

» Observe the terrain ahead. Are there any dead spaces (unforeseen roadblocks and other unknown obstacles)?

» Complete a good route reconnaissance – observe the area for "enemy" locations or determine where interactions may occur. Identify areas where you may come into contact with others.
» Understand that the route you take may require some special equipment, skills, guidance, and/or support from others.

When you look for the best route to make it to your objective, the path you choose may not be the easiest, quickest, or the one that initially seems to be perfect. Things change – there's always a possibility you'll need to modify the original plan. That's why you always want to choose at least three routes.

» The **Primary Route (PR)** is the best route – the way you believe will best support your movement toward the objective.
» The **Alternative Route (AR)** is a good option if you can't use the PR for some reason. It might take almost the same amount of time, but maybe there will be a few more obstacles or chances of traffic.
» The **Contingency Route (CR)** will get you to where you need to go, but it's the least desirable – it may take longer or not allow the best view ahead, but it's a path you can use if needed.

Three Routes Example: Driving to an Interview

When Joanne is driving to her next interview, she could prepare three routes to ensure she arrives on time and with the least amount of frustration possible. Her Primary Route (PR) takes the interstate. If her PR becomes too congested, stressful, or even if she just gets tired of the pace of traffic and feels like she's becoming distracted, she'll have several options she can use.

One option is to pull over at a rest area and check the GPS on her phone. This is like the Range Card's Target Reference Points (TRPs), milestones where you can pause to reference your Magnetic North. Remember, TRPs allow you to check where you are in relationship to your goals, and your Magnetic North keeps you focused on who you are. Are you staying focused on your goals or are you beginning to feel lost in the mud?

When Joanne pulls over, she needs to answer some questions honestly: Am I on the right road? Am I (still) traveling in the right direction? Is this route still the best way to my destination? Am I traveling too fast, getting ahead of myself? How is my vehicle doing? Do I need to get fuel and make a phone call? Or do I just need to rest for a bit, gather my thoughts, stretch my legs, and take a minute to be thankful I've gotten as far as I have safely?

After she's checked her GPS, she can decide to alter or modify her PR and continue, or she can look at and compare her PR to her Alternate Route (AR). Is the AR still viable? Would this be a good time to consider changing course and switching to the AR? The answer may be a clear yes or no, or "we'll see." No worries, Joanne can continue to move ahead and observe where she is and where she intends to go.

Joanne's Alternate Route is a combination of secondary state and local roads. I'm sure you're familiar with how hectic and congested most major interstates can be. When and where there is trouble on the roads, there may be accidents, lane closures, road debris, and the occasional rude driver who thinks they're more important than everyone else, weaving in and out of traffic – cutting others off, often creating hazardous and potentially deadly driving conditions.

So if Joanne begins to feel nervous, she can pull over, re-evaluate her PR, look at the AR, and decide which would work best for her. There is no penalty for taking time to assess where you are. The key is not to sit and become stagnant with what is known as "analysis paralysis," where you spend so much time overanalyzing, nothing gets done.

Check your map, check your routes, assess where you are, make decisions, and move out.

Joanne's Contingency Route (CR) is made up of side streets, back roads, detours, and full of traffic lights. It's not her preferred route, and it might take longer, but it will get her to her interview safely and on time.

 It's better to have and not need than to need and not have.

Cover

In the military, cover gives you protection from the enemy's sight and/or fire; it could be a wall, vehicle, or anything that could stop a bullet. Cover means the enemy might know where you are, but if they try to engage, they cannot "hit" you. If you have to move from one position to another, you want to move from a covered and/or concealed position to another covered/concealed position.

Even if your business or personal life might make you feel as if you're dodging bullets sometimes, you can still find cover – but hiding under the bed like a dog afraid of thunderstorms won't work! Cover might include colleagues or friends who can provide support, having resources you'll need collected ahead of time, or any other part of preparation that could shield you from potential issues or obstacles. You can build cover by developing your social and professional networks and by making sure you have the tools to succeed.

The way lawyers prepare for trial is a good example of building cover. The defense can anticipate arguments the prosecuting lawyer may make and prepare ways to discredit, redirect, or otherwise make those arguments powerless in front of a jury; they might collect evidence, witness testimonies, and other resources ahead of time. Whether or not the prosecution can "see" them there, if the defense lawyer can produce contradictory evidence or convince the judge to disallow a certain line of questioning, the prosecution can't "hit" them.

You must prepare for your journey. Like the defense lawyer, you must consider where you want to start, where you want to take the testimony, and what resources you'll need along the way.

Concealment

Concealment is different from cover. Where cover provides protection, concealment just conceals your position – but it also allows you to observe what is happening around you. Concealment can be as simple as listening in a meeting to gain knowledge and learn from others.

Obstacles

Sometimes the hardest part of planning is being able to identify what's an obstacle and what's just a bump in the road that might slow you down a bit. Identifying potential obstacles before you begin a project allows you to look at areas of concern, areas you'll have to assess, address, and prepare for.

Start by looking at what has held you back or created a hurdle in the past. Some obstacles we face are of our own making. It's hard to admit it, but in many cases, we can be our most difficult obstacle to overcome (trust me, I know). If you're in a new or unfamiliar situation, you may also want to talk to someone who has been somewhere similar or pursued the same goal, since they'll probably have some helpful insight and lessons learned to share.

Key Terrain

Key terrain refers to areas that could give an advantage if taken by an attacker or defender. Controlling terrain doesn't mean you need to be territorial or defensive; it just means you need to be able to see where and when interactions may take place. You want to choose the best place for you to be successful. Through the control of key terrain, you will be able to engage others in a more positive and results-orientated manner.

Do you really want the boss to hit you up in the break room for a surprise update on that project, or would you rather schedule a quick five-minute meeting ahead of time, so you're prepared? Key terrain can be many spaces within an organization: the coffee/break room, individual offices, shop floor, company functions, monthly meeting – basically anywhere you might interact with others.

Who controls key terrain controls the battle.

Sometimes determining the best place for you to be successful may also include knowing how your colleagues communicate or where they are personally, so interpersonal skills and empathy are important here. For example, after you set a task in your project management system, will your colleagues benefit from a quick chat to reiterate or clarify what's needed, and to answer some questions they might have? Do you need to remember that a specific colleague often sends really short, to-the-point emails, so it might be better to get their input on something over the phone? Or if you have an idea to present, and your project lead has been in back-to-back meetings all day, your key terrain is probably sometime the next day when they can take a fresh look at it and might not be so stressed and worn out from the day's activities.

Let's look at an example. You have a weekly In Progress Review meeting where each department gives an update on what they have going on, what is expected or going to be accomplished, and to discuss any requirements to support day-to-day operations. Think about how these meetings usually go. Do you feel they serve value? How do other members feel about the meeting? Is it a safe space to share ideas and feedback? Or do things occasionally get tense between attendees?

The weekly meeting would be the key terrain; it's identifiable as an area of engagement and an area to be observed. If someone shares an idea you think is completely unattainable, you'll need to decide if this is the key terrain where you want to engage, based on your experience with the meetings and the current situation at the organization. Would it be beneficial to "shoot down" their suggestion then and there, or would it be better to listen (concealment) and have the facts and figures available (cover) to support your position at a later time? Perhaps in a brainstorming session limited to your department?

I'm not trying to suggest you should always have your guard up, but remember there are times and places where interactions should and will take place. You just need to be prepared and have a plan.

Avenues of Approach

How do you get to key terrain? By an Avenue of Approach. As you move toward your goals, you've looked at potential routes and planned where you want to go – you've established a path. Now you just need to make sure you have the best means of traveling that path based on your review of terrain – you need to choose an Avenue of Approach.

In the military, Avenues of Approach are an air or ground route of an attacking force leading to its objective or key terrain. Since Avenues of Approach detail the way you achieve your goals, this could be your planning guidelines or the mindset you adopt – so some Avenues of Approach may not work as well. For instance, have you ever felt stuck in a reactive mindset? No matter how hard you work, it can feel like you're always playing catch up, and every time you have to respond, your patience grows shorter. It'll be hard to reach your goals with this mindset. Take the time to pause and reflect on the avenues available to you. How do you wish to approach a problem or an opportunity?

Your path, route reconnaissance, and goal planning process will show you how you want to get to your destination.

Approaching your objective can take time as you move along your route, and you have to be ready to change paths, navigate obstacles, and engage others, but you should also know when to slow down and check the map to make sure you're still on the best path to your objective. Remind yourself, as I often remind myself: "Try to be patient – after all, this is a journey."

OCOKA Example: Being Intentional in Your Career

We often don't have as many opportunities as we'd like to just sit and reflect on our bigger goals and life pursuits, like establishing a clear career path. Maybe you're still figuring out a direction, or maybe your career has felt like it's been on autopilot since your last promotion, but whatever the case, you need to assess where you are and be honest with yourself in your professional capacity.

Let's say Ralph was so impressed by how well the OODA Loop worked to save his barbecue, he talked to Joanne about other planning techniques he could try. Like Joanne, he's been working with the same company for a while and wants to find ways to progress – he just doesn't have an interest in moving up any further in the ranks right now. Instead, he wants to find ways to grow professionally without taking on more managerial responsibilities.

Questions and Considerations

When reflecting on work and setting goals for progression, Ralph might start by *observing* where he is with questions like:

- » Am I happy doing what I'm doing? Am I happy at my workplace, considering management, expectations, and company culture?
- » Do I want to advance toward a position of greater responsibility and leadership? Would I need to leave my current employment to achieve a higher position?
- » Do I want to progress laterally or by taking on a new area of responsibility, without a manager role?
- » Is the industry I'm in undergoing changes that will affect my position? Is it possible technology could replace me?
- » Can I master the newer technologies? If I need to learn new applications, how will I do this?
- » Do I feel like I have a future with my organization?

Ralph's OCOKA

Observation

I love working at a tutoring and learning development organization, but I don't necessarily love everything I do for my job. When I first started, I mainly worked one-on-one with students. Since an exciting promotion a few months ago, more of my job involves management and overseeing colleagues who do what I used to do.

I love passing on what I've learned and advocating for the people I manage – which makes sense, because I find teaching so rewarding. The hardest and least fulfilling part of my job now involves selling our services to potential customers. I know if I continue moving up in the company, that will become more and more of what I do, which makes me feel a little stuck in my current role. How can I continue developing professionally in a different way?

Primary Route	I have an opportunity to lead a training session for new hires. I'm hoping I could lead more of these in the future and possibly contribute more to training development. I've invited the person who is the head of our training department, Parker, to sit in on one of the sessions I'll lead to offer constructive feedback.

Ralph's OCOKA

Alternative Route	If Parker can't make it, she said her associate head will attend one of the sessions. I know I can still get good feedback, but Parker's impression of my work will be filtered through someone else.
Contingency Route	My company offers internal development courses, but I'd rather use them to bolster what I'm doing than have them be the focus. I don't feel like these courses alone will help me progress, but they could help me learn more about our training department and slowly contribute more.

Cover

I've been taking an online course about teaching and lesson planning for adults, since I have more experience teaching kids. I've also been collecting feedback from those I manage for the last month or so to find out how I can better support them, which I think will help me look for opportunities and gaps during training sessions.

Concealment

It's been a while since I was onboarded as tutor, so I asked Parker if I could sit in on an upcoming session. This means I'll be able to get familiar with the content and lesson structure again, and I'll be able to see her in action.

Ralph's OCOKA

Obstacles

- » I need to be trained to lead the training session – more of a bump than an obstacle.
- » I know from past experiences that I have a lot of anxiety about being misunderstood when teaching adults. Kids are quicker to ask questions, repeat back what you've said, and ask for clarification. Many adults hesitate to ask what they think might be a "stupid" question.
- » I worry my management responsibilities might not leave enough time for me to be involved with more of these training sessions.

Key Terrain

I don't want to bombard Parker with questions whenever we run into each other in the hallway – she's really busy! But I know I can reach out if I ever want to set a meeting for feedback or to talk about our training program. My bi-monthly one-on-ones with my manager will be a good place to discuss my development and opportunities to contribute to the training department.

Avenues of Approach

I think it's really important – for myself and those I teach – to keep a growth mindset. I try to focus on gains (progress made) rather than gaps (distance between where I am and want to be). I know I can continue to adjust my professional development plans as I progress, so I'm going to set benchmarks to regularly review this OCOKA plan and update.

Getting from A to B: Primary, Alternate, Contingency, Emergency (PACE) Planning

Primary Goal/Usage: PACE is a Course of Action planning model – so if you know you'll need a backup plan or two, this technique will help.

Time to Complete: 15 minutes to a few days, depending on the depth, detail, and size of a goal.

What's PACE Planning?

PACE represents Primary, Alternate, Contingency, and Emergency Planning. Each type of plan is based on another and needs to support the goal, task, and/or objective. This is a good planning technique if you know you'll need a solid backup plan, especially if you might also need a backup plan for your backup plan.

Don't forget to share your action plans with team members or others involved with reaching your goal. Everyone on the team needs to know the plan and be familiar with it in

> ## Key Terms
>
> » A **Primary Plan (PP)** is the best plan, which will use the best methodology and thus give the best results.
> » An **Alternate Plan (AP)** is developed alongside the Primary Plan (PP) to support it if anything goes wrong; it remains fairly close to the PP, with only some minor variation.
> » A **Contingency Plan (CP)** is a plan that's very different from the Primary or Alternative Plan, but that still supports the overall goal.
> » An **Emergency Plan (EP)** is the plan when everything else has gone out the window. It's the best you can do given circumstances that greatly disrupted the situation.

case something changes. This sharing and collaboration also makes the team stronger, more knowledgeable, and more operationally efficient.

Primary, Alternate, Contingency, and Emergency Plans

Primary Plan

The initial plan you choose to follow is known as the Primary Plan. This is your best plan, the one where your resources, planning, and efforts will have the very best chance of success. This plan is the one you feel will use the best methodology and thus yield the best results. The Primary Plan is what you want to do and how you want to do it.

But what if the Primary Plan doesn't work, or what if the situation changes? What if you are thrown a proverbial curve ball? Don't panic – you have an Alternate Plan.

Alternate Plan

How many times have you watched a perfect, well-thought-out plan collapse – perhaps not so much because of anything you did or didn't do, but because something fell through? How did you react? Did you panic? Or did you just throw a secondary plan together and hope for the best? What if you had developed that plan ahead of time, so if the Primary Plan didn't work out, you could just pivot to the Alternate Plan at critical coordination points?

For example, imagine you're preparing recommendations for a new project at work. If your Primary Plan involves gathering recommendations and data from Cathy, you may want to check if Brenda and Joe can help if Cathy runs out of bandwidth. If your manager is away just before you share your findings, you might setup a time to review considerations and requirements before they leave in case there's no time before your presentation.

When the Primary Plan has to be modified, you need to look at the Alternate Plan. The Alternate Plan is developed alongside the Primary Plan to support it if anything goes wrong; it remains fairly close to the Primary Plan, and with only some minor variations, people can quickly adapt to the Alternate Plan if or when the situation changes.

Contingency Plan

Let's go a little deeper and think about what you would do if your best attempts at planning failed. What if your Primary Plan and Alternate Plan were both Overcome-By-Events (OBE'ed)? Even if you have a plan and a backup plan, things happen. A Contingency Plan is a different plan, perhaps with different steps and a different pathway, but it still supports the overall goal.

In the military we always developed Contingency Plans, and local governments as well as many businesses develop all kinds of CPs for a variety of potential events (flood, fire, earthquake, pandemic, etc.). When the COVID-19 pandemic suddenly shut down much of the world, business owners with pandemic Contingency Plans were able to quickly communicate to employees the situation and how the company would approach it. Those who didn't have a CP may have scrambled to find digital communication and project management tools to support employees who'd never been remote before. They may have also struggled initially with communication and visibility after such a shift in how work was done, without normal in-person meetings and opportunities for impromptu check-ins in the kitchen.

A Contingency Plan allows you to continue to function and accomplish your goals, despite unforeseeable circumstances.

Emergency Plan

An Emergency Plan is for when something happens that makes the Primary, Alternate, and Contingency Plans ineffective, and you may have to make decisions or changes to the plan on-the-spot. Naturally, this is not a good place to be, but you can still plan and prepare as part of our planning techniques. The Emergency Plan allows for the basic functions, goals, and objectives of the original plan to hopefully be met and accomplished. This is sometimes done by taking the do-able portions of the Primary, Alternate, and Contingency Plans, stitching them together, making adjustments, briefing the team, and then enacting the Emergency Plan.

The Emergency Plan is not intended for a long-term solution to an event. It can give you some breathing room to continue to assess and plan for the next objective or to give you enough time to modify and adjust your Primary Plan – which then, of course, will feed into the Alternate and Contingency Plans.

Reflection in PACE Planning

Remember when we talked about constantly assessing your position (Range Card, OODA)? Checking your map and your routes (OCOKA)? Well, after completing a goal, it's still useful to look back on the planning process. What were your Primary and Alternate Plans? Did you take the time to create a Contingency Plan too? Did you need to call on your Alternate and Contingency Plans? How well did they support your Primary Plan? Knowing what you know now, could they have been acted upon? What would you change, modify, adjust, and/or leave in place?

You can manage and control many things in your life. You don't have to – nor should you – leave things to chance or luck. Neither always go your way. By having Primary, Alternate, Contingency, and Emergency Plans available to implement when needed, you'll feel a bit more confident and ready for what life may throw at you.

You may have heard the phrase before, "The best laid plans of mice and men often go awry." It's usually quoted when something goes wrong, and it comes from a Scots-language poem by Robert Burns, apologizing to a mouse whose nest has been overturned by a plow:

> "But Mousie, thou art no thy-lane,
> In proving foresight may be vain:
> The best laid schemes o' Mice an' Men
>   Gang aft agley,
> An' lea'e us nought but grief an' pain,
>   For promis'd joy!
> Still, thou art blest, compar'd wi' me!
> The present only toucheth thee:
> But Och! I backward cast my e'e,
>   On prospects drear!
> An' forward tho' I canna see,
>   I guess an' fear!"[2]

What Burns is saying is that no matter how much you plan, you can still have some problems. Simply put, sometimes the feces still hits the rotating blades.

---

[2] Burns, Robert. "Poems and Songs of Robert Burns, by Robert Burns." *Project Gutenberg*, www.gutenberg.org. Accessed 11 Apr. 2022.

PACE Planning Example: Revisiting Promotion and Progression

After Joanne didn't get the promotion, she reviewed how her interview went and began making plans for continued progression by using the PVC-E technique. Since then, she's continued supporting the intern program at her job, and she's enjoyed helping her friend Ralph learn about planning techniques and begin working on his own progression.

As she looks ahead, Joanne wants to create a plan for her own future that's easier to quickly adjust – so if another opportunity for a promotion comes up, she'll be prepared to succeed or pivot as needed.

Joanne's PACE Planning

Primary Plan

The Primary Plan I started creating with the PVC-E technique focused on continuing to support the intern program, working on my learning/development plan, and finding other ways to contribute and develop my leadership skills.

My manager and I agreed to be accountability buddies to make sure I didn't miss as many of my classes, and in the last few months, he's recommended me for a project team lead and intern training opportunities to develop and showcase my leadership skills. My colleague who got the promotion, Mary, shared some helpful resources with me, and she knows I can help with her team if she ever needs a hand. I also determined that I needed to practice interviewing more so I would feel confident from the beginning of an interview.

Since my company is still actively hiring more staff in my current position, I know that a similar promotion to lead a small team will be coming up in the next 6 months.

Joanne's PACE Planning

Alternate Plan

My Alternate Plan will be very similar to my Primary Plan, but I need to be prepared for some changes that might be happening in the near future.

I know my manager and his wife want to grow their family, so it's possible he will be going on paternity leave for a few months. When that happens, I would be reporting to a different manager – who may not be as interested or experienced in supporting someone's professional development. That means I would lose my accountability buddy and a great mentor for a while, but I also wouldn't have someone who can advocate for me and highlight my work to our department and the leadership team.

I've talked to Mary about this, and she agreed having a great manager can make a big difference in an employee's development and progression. Since she's pulled me in to help with training her team, I've begun developing a good rapport with her manager – who's also a great mentor. I know Mary's manager would help coach and advocate for me if my manager does go on leave.

Joanne's PACE Planning

Contingency Plan

If both my Primary and Alternate Plans run into immovable obstacles, my Contingency Plan takes a page out of Ralph's book – I can work on lateral progression.

After I didn't get the last promotion, I reminded myself why I wanted it in the first place: to support others the way my managers have helped me in the past. Working with our intern program more has been an enlightening and rewarding experience, and the leaders of the program have told me how much they appreciate my help.

If I need a new plan, or even if it begins to feel like my Primary or Alternate Plan will take much longer than I'd hoped, I can apply to formally join the department that manages our intern program. The positions I'd be eligible for wouldn't really be a promotion from my current role, just a sideways move, but I'd be able to coach interns and help them progress in their new careers. Plus, along with gaining leadership experience, I'd learn more about other departments at my company – which could make other opportunities more viable for me in the future.

Joanne's PACE Planning

Emergency Plan

If my Primary, Alternate, and Contingency Plans won't work, I'll need an Emergency Plan to help me pivot or at least provide some time to rework my PACE Planning.

I've always preferred the idea of sticking with the same company for a long time, even though I know it's become more typical to work for multiple companies over your career. But if my job starts to feel like it's heading for a dead end, to continue progressing and growing, I can start looking for positions at other companies.

To make this possible, I need to make sure I'm keeping my resume and LinkedIn profile updated, especially as I complete training courses and develop more experience. I've also started contributing to my company's blog – with a byline – and making sure I share the posts on LinkedIn. These are two important assets I'll have ready if I need to enact my Emergency Plan, and I know I can continue to focus on developing them as I look for a new job.

Chaos Management: Mission, Equipment, Troops, Time Available (METT) - Terrain, Civilians, Politics (TCP)

Primary Goal/Usage: METT-TCP helps you gain a deeper understanding of a goal, how success will be defined, and any holistic considerations needed – like how your actions may be viewed by others or how those close to you might be indirectly affected as you work toward the objective.

Time to Complete: 10-15 minutes

What's METT-TCP?

METT-TCP stands for: Mission, Equipment, Troops, Time Available; and Terrain, Civilians, and Political Considerations. It might sound like a lot, but it really isn't. As with all the techniques we've discussed, METT-TCP helps you gain more clarity as it moves you toward a deeper understanding of what you'll need to accomplish your task or mission and how you'll define success.

Key Terms

- The **Mission** is the goal you're trying to accomplish.
- **Equipment** is resources needed to complete a task.
- **Troops** are the people supporting or working on a goal together.
- **Time Available** is how much time you have to complete a task or goal.
- **Terrain** (referred to as Key Terrain in other techniques) are areas that could give you an advantage.
- **Civilians (On The Battlefield)** are people in your life who may not be directly involved with a goal but will influence and/or be affected by your pursuit of it.
- **Political Considerations** review how your actions, results, and capabilities will be viewed by others.

Mission

You need to ask yourself: What's my mission? What do I need to accomplish? You have to know this before you can do anything else.

I find that a short, well-written mission statement is most helpful. It tells me what has to be done, sets parameters for tasks, and shows me the direction I should go. I also need to know if my mission is tied to others, or if other people will have missions tied into mine. Am I able to start my task now, or do I have to wait for someone else to accomplish their tasks first? If I know what I have to do, I can move on to the next question.

Equipment

What equipment or resources are needed to complete this task? Will I need to acquire necessary items from outside sources, or do I have them on hand?

I know sometimes the equipment you need is sort of obvious — for example, a shovel to clear the sidewalk after a snowstorm. But what are some other types of equipment you might need to make sure the sidewalk is safe? Maybe a scraper would help with tough sections of ice, and you could use sand for patches you can't remove. What about clothing? Along with a coat, you'll probably want gloves, a hat, and boots. Having a list of equipment might seem like too much for such an ordinary task, but it can help you make sure you don't forget something important – and I know I'd rather have the sand in my garage *before* the snowstorm hits.

After the Mission (or task) is completed and I'm done using the equipment, what do I do with it? Do I need to clean anything or move it to storage? If there is a lot of equipment involved, who is going to move it? This brings us to the next aspect of METT-TCP.

Troops

If your task is complex or requires a few extra hands, get the troops out there! But first, you must communicate what you need them to do, how you want them to accomplish it, and the desired result. Do they just need to shovel the walk? Or do they need to make sure it's thoroughly scraped and sprinkled with sand? If Grandma needs to be able to safely walk to the door during her upcoming visit, your desired results may be different than in normal circumstances.

Communicating the plan is essential. What good is the best of plans if no one knows about it? You can share the plan verbally (in person, on a call) or in writing (by text, email, messaging app, etc.) to inform the troops. You also need to make sure the troops have the resources, knowledge, and skills to be successful.

The ability to ask for help is an essential skill. You can't always do everything. Everyone needs support sometimes, and you need troops to help you succeed. Even master chefs have a sous chef and other assistants to help prepare and serve meals. Having qualified and skilled troops can greatly increase the probability of mission success, so always consider if your mission would be easier or more successful with help – and don't be afraid to ask for it.

Time Available

Now that you've rallied the troops behind your mission, you need to consider timing. When do you need to complete your mission? How much time do you have?

If you know when a task must be done, you can start reverse planning to work out an accurate mission start time. You do this all the time, you just might not be aware there's a fancy label for it. You start with a deadline and work backwards, visualizing the steps and time needed to complete each action or task.

For example, if you need to be at work by 8am, and the drive is 20 minutes from the house to the office, then you know you have to leave by 7:30am – leaving a 10 minute window for what is commonly referred to as "the fudge factor" or "allowing time for Murphy to show up." This ten-minute window gives you buffer time so you don't have to rush, and it allows for red lights and snarled traffic. That's reverse planning – knowing when a task needs to be accomplished, the approximate time the task will take, subtracting the difference, and determining the start time.

Time can be affected by many factors, but some that will affect METT-TCP are task dependencies and equipment availability. If you need others to complete tasks prior to beginning yours, your task is dependent on theirs. Thus, their lack of planning can greatly impact whether or not you are successful. If you know this will be the case, since you addressed the issue in your Mission considerations, it's wise to know who is doing what and when they need to finish it. Depending on the individual, you may have to shepherd this process along, making sure they're on track.

If you know your mission is dependent on others, you must let them know. As long as you're polite about it, most people will appreciate you being candid about this – they don't want to feel like they're holding someone else up. Plus, you don't want to be blamed for a failure or delay. If you sense that your timeline may be compromised, let your supervisor know. Don't just wait and hope for the best, and most importantly, don't compromise your schedule because someone else didn't use proper planning and management techniques. (Thank goodness you're reading this book! Maybe they should read it too?) Be ready with a factual, honest, and objective assessment of why your piece of a larger task may be at risk.

Time can also be dramatically affected by the availability of equipment. How long can you have the equipment? When will it be ready? Will it be delivered to you, or will you have to go get it?

Time is an important factor in the planning process. It's a critical resource that, once lost, cannot be recovered. That's why time management is so critical. Instead of losing it due to poor planning, you could *gain* time and insight by planning and managing it. Assess the time factor in what you do each day. Explore the reasons you feel rushed. Simply put: if you are rushed, look at *why* you are rushed. Determine what you and your time are really worth. As you begin to better manage your time, you'll find that you have more of it to utilize the most important of all your resources: YOU!

After receiving or issuing the mission, acquiring the equipment, communicating the plan to the troops, and applying a realistic timeline, you're all set to look at a topic we've covered several times now, including in the OCOKA and PACE techniques.

Terrain

Terrain is the lay of the land in front, behind, and around you. As with the Range Card, you have to look at what you can see, develop your route to the objective, and get a sense of what could assist or hinder you in accomplishing your tasks. Terrain can affect what type of equipment you'll need, the timeline you've developed, and how many troops you'll receive and of what quality. Most importantly, terrain is unforgiving. It generally won't bend to you, so it's best to use terrain to your advantage. Stay on the high ground – the view is better.

When assessing terrain, you need to identify what the best key terrain is. If you're forced into a defensive position, where is the best place to be? As you move toward mission completion, what and where will your points of reference – which tell you if you are on the correct path or deviating from your chosen route – be on the terrain?

Terrain tells you if you'll have to cross streams, rail lines, roads, rivers, valleys, mountains, molehills, etc. Where are the best and safest places to cross? If you need to rest, where would be a good spot to pause and assess where you are in your journey?

If the terrain is slowing you down, what will you do? Where will you go for assistance and guidance? Many times we get lost or disoriented about who we are, what we want from life, and where we are going. We often forget this is normal. How many times have you driven somewhere and gotten a little (okay, maybe a lot) lost? I know I have.

When you get lost, it makes sense to ask for directions. Guidance may come from reflection, a respected colleague's advice, speaking with your life partner, asking a spiritual leader; or just laying down, looking at the ceiling, and letting your mind wander. It's never too late to develop or revise your vision for the future.

The important point is to know where you want to go and then make a plan. That's the essence of this book – planning and managing who you are, where you want to go, and how you want to get there.

Civilians On The Battlefield (COTB)

This consideration of the METT-TCP process has recently been added, but it does make good sense. Civilians On The Battlefield (COTB) represent the people in your life who may not be directly involved with the goal you're working towards, but who will influence and/or be affected by your planning process, how it's going, and the outcome. They may not be part of your troops, but they can still have a big impact on reaching your goal.

In a project at work, COTB may be colleagues who can offer guidance or contribute to resource gathering. Do you need additional people to help? What about specific skill sets or talents which could make projects go more smoothly? On the other hand, COTB may be coworkers you just need to avoid during a part of the process. Who or what might negatively impact your project? Is there one colleague who's enthusiastic to help with planning but just drags out the process? Would it be beneficial to *not* get a specific person's feedback until you're at least on the second iteration? In the personal areas of your life, you probably already know what or who brings drama to the table and stresses you out – people you really don't need around to add to your confusion.

But COTB may also be the people who need your help in other areas of life – people around you who may be affected by your plan. For example, if your plan focuses on business or professional development, how will it affect your family? How does your plan prepare them for the longer hours and greater energy you'll expend at work? How will home operations continue smoothly, and how will you adjust other parts of your schedule (e.g., hobbies, etc.) to prioritize family time?

If you get better at identifying those COTB, you can begin to avoid the chaos they may bring to your situation and encourage order, quiet, and stability in your workplace and home (even with young children). As you get better at identifying the traits of the COTB that bring stress to your life, you can avoid those stresses. I know I would rather have peace and serenity around me. So you need to identify the COTB who assist you, those who will help you find fulfillment in other areas of life, and those you need to avoid.

Political Considerations

Everything that happens – everything you do or plan to do – creates ripples in your life. Most of them are pretty small, but remember that you're not the only one splashing around. If life is like a pond, there are always ripples out there banging into other ripples, creating waves.

Since you don't move in a vacuum, you need to think about how your actions, results, and capabilities will be viewed by others. This is a critical point of METT-TCP. In your professional and personal lives, you have to work with others, and they have to work with you. You need to be able to rely on others' talents, skills, and dedication as much as they rely on yours. If something may happen that could negatively impact your relationship with your troops or anyone supporting your goal, you need to be able to proactively acknowledge and deal with the issue.

For example, imagine you're planning a co-working event with the members of your project team. It's an important opportunity for you to collaborate in person, so you want to add it to the first open day on the team calendar – but that happens to be a Wednesday. Since you're aware one team member can't usually get childcare then, you reach out to him to discuss adjusting schedules to find a different day, helping him find care options, or simply bringing his child to work that day if preferred. With that one chat, you find a solution and ensure your colleague doesn't feel overlooked or unimportant.

Part of the planning and managing process is recognizing the political considerations, working with them, and ensuring you address issues and support those working with you.

Conducting a METT-TCP Assessment

Conducting a strong, honest METT-TCP analysis will help you manage the chaos and gain a better understanding of where you are and where you're going. As you fill in each consideration, be specific – don't be too general or vague, since details will allow you to better plan and understand what's happening. By being specific, you'll actually begin to formulate a general plan of action, which you can expand and develop into a specific, goal-orientated plan you can follow and articulate to others.

Remember to be honest. No one has to know your answers, and there's no one looking over your shoulder. If you don't want to share this exercise with anyone, you don't need to. Let your thoughts flow freely. There is no right or wrong answer, just you taking a moment with yourself.

Questions and Considerations

- **Mission:** What's your goal? What are you trying to do?
- **Equipment:** What resources will you need? Do you have a list?
- **Troops:** Do you need any help? Who will be completing tasks to support your mission?
- **Time Available:** When must this task be completed? Have you set a realistic timeline? Do you have enough time available to complete the tasks needed to accomplish the mission?
- **Terrain:** What's in front of you? Obstacles, reference points, places of engagement, etc.? What path do you want to take?
- **Civilians (On the Battlefield):** Who's with you? Who will be affected by your pursuit of the mission – allies, opponents, people who will support you, et al.?
- **Political Considerations:** What could the impacts be of enacting your plan to accomplish the mission? What might you need to consider related to other people involved or impacted?

Now that you've worked through these questions, look over what you've written. You can highlight the most important points for each area of METT-TCP and note down a succinct list to guide you along the way. Keep your original answers to provide more context while completing the mission and to go back over during your analysis later. This is also a good exercise for you to develop a clearer set of mental check points and bring some order to the chaos. Try to analyze each of your responses for clarity.

Remember, impacts and considerations can come from everywhere. Be aware of your surroundings, the people with you, and the political impacts/considerations of what you will or won't want to do.

METT-TCP Example: The VIP Tour

Ralph was chosen to lead a tour at the tutoring center, and he's excited because some important people will be attending! Along with the CEO of the company, there will be a few celebrity parents who are considering the tutoring services offered by the company. Ralph knows he needs to make a good impression, highlight safety measures in place, and give the parents an idea of what lessons are like – even though it'll be after hours, when no classes are in session. After working through the questions above, Ralph writes out his plan.

Ralph's METT-TCP

Mission

» Conduct a tour for VIPs at the tutoring center. The tour must be conducted safely and efficiently from entrance to exit from the site.
» The goal is for everyone on the tour to be impressed by how much our employees care and are invested in their work, while addressing any concerns by showing the site is safe and operating well.

Equipment

» A room available for the briefing at the beginning and any questions after the tour.
» Special badges to identify VIPs (since they'll be at the center outside normal business hours).
» Radios to communicate with security/parking attendants.
» A list of confirmed attendees, printed the afternoon of the tour in case anyone needs to cancel last minute.
» Designated parking near the entrance, blocked off earlier in the day to ensure VIPs don't need to park far away. An additional two spots should also be saved for staff closing at the end of normal operating hours.

Ralph's METT-TCP

Troops

We'll need three other team members to support the tour:

- One team member stationed near the entrance to unlock the door and guide VIPs to the meeting room. They'll also coordinate with the security team that monitors the building (but not our suite specifically).
- Another team member will assist me with the tour. They'll help answer questions and make sure no one falls behind.
- A third team member has agreed to be available in case any attendees need childcare during the tour.

Time Available

- We've allotted two hours for the tour and questions.
- The center closes at 6pm, and we need to lock up by 9pm. This allows time for the tour, 30 minutes extra in case we go over, and another 30 minutes to finish closing once the VIPs have left.
- We've blocked out 5-6pm on our schedules so we can finish setting up and make sure everything is in place before the VIPs arrive.

Terrain

- The tour will progress from the entrance and around the main, U-shaped hallway. Then we'll return to the meeting room for Q&A.
- We should avoid rooms B and C, which are having renovations done after there were issues with the roof.
- I haven't led this tour before, but I assisted with a similar tour last month to confirm how long it might take and determine if there might be any obstacles.

Ralph's METT-TCP

Civilians (On The Battlefield)

- » Some attendees may be coming straight from work, so we'll have sandwiches and snacks available as they arrive.
- » Since many of our VIPs are potential customers, we have arranged for a team member to provide childcare.
- » The Center Director will be in her office. She usually stays after closing on Wednesdays, and the meeting room is near her office, so we need to try not to disturb her.
- » We've confirmed that other offices at the site will be okay with us reserving parking spaces later in the day.
- » Our building is already optimized for accessibility, and we've communicated our setup to all attendees to make sure no one's worried about feeling excluded or overlooked.

Political Considerations

- » If the tour is successful, we could have new students soon – meaning we'll have more hours to offer our staff.
- » Because this is a VIP tour, some of the students' parents could be important advocates for the work we do.
- » We know reserving parking spaces may be annoying for people who work in other offices in the building, so we sent each office a thank you note with a gift card to buy their team doughnuts.

Clarifying the Operation: Tasks, Conditions, and Standards

> **Primary Goal/Usage:** Tasks, Conditions, and Standards is a quick technique to check a plan and understand what's needed. This technique is helpful for communicating an operation to others.
>
> **Time to Complete:** 5-10 minutes

What are Tasks, Conditions, and Standards?

These three words can meet any situation that is chaotic, unclear, or needs to be explained to others. It's simple:

- » What do you need to do?
- » What are the resources you have available, and what constraints are you operating under?
- » To what level do you need to accomplish your task to be judged successful?

Think about how this can be applied to your personal, professional, and social activities. How could these three

> ## Key Terms
>
> » **Tasks** are exactly what needs to be done – the goal or objective itself and any related or dependent duties.
> » **Conditions** are the constraints you'll operate under. These could be the resources you'll have or need.
> » **Standards** are specifications or variables used to define success.

words make a difference when talking to your spouse, partner, children, friends, family, coworkers – anyone and everyone you interact with? Tasks, Conditions, and Standards help you clearly define what needs to be done, how to do it, and how success will be defined.

Tasks

You need to identify exactly what you need to do. What's your objective, your goal? What tasks need to be accomplished to meet your goal? Are there sub-tasks to be completed? Without knowing what you need to do, how can you do it?

Communicating with others about what needs to be done takes time to master. How often does it seem you're asked to do something and you really don't know what it is you're supposed to be doing? You need to learn how to ask for guidance and how to provide clear instructions to others. Be patient with yourself; this is a learning process.

Ask yourself, "What task do I need to accomplish?" Once the task has been established, it can be processed out into smaller, more manageable goals. All goals require steps to achieve them.

Remember: Small steps start great journeys.

Conditions

Once you've determined what you need to do, you have to look at the conditions in which you'll complete your tasks. Conditions are the constraints you'll be operating under.

Conditions can be the resources you will have or need. Some basic conditions that could influence your ability to complete a task include:

» Funding
» Personnel available
» Equipment available
» Time available
» Dependence on others' timelines and completion of their tasks
» Political considerations

Ask yourself: "What are the conditions under which I have to operate?" Then add them to the list.

Standards

A standard is something by which an event, activity, task, or project is judged to be successful. Success can be defined by many variables – quality, rate of completion, gains or progress made, and so on.

Often the person who assigns a task (Tasker) must set the standard for the person or people doing the task (Taskee). When you set a standard of success, you need to remind yourself a standard must be realistic, clearly defined, quantifiable, and achievable. Setting high standards is perfectly acceptable if you know the Taskee can meet the applied and established standard, even when the "Taskee" is you.

Standards are funny things; they can often be modified and moved about. If standards are not met, but everything has been done right, you have to determine why. Were the standards set too high? Is there an issue with resourcing, training, time constraints, and/or funding? If you determine any reason for the standards not being met, you must address it. If everyone is meeting the minimum, should you evaluate the standards and perhaps raise them?

On a personal level, what standards do you have in your life? What defines success for you? Are there certain standards you will not compromise on? Are there standards you apply to others? What happens when your standards are not met? What can you do to meet them?

The Right to Clarity

You have a responsibility and a right to clarity in the tasks and goals you pursue in life. You have a right to ask for clarification about the tasks, conditions, and standards that will guide a project. You have a responsibility to yourself and – most importantly – to others to clarify what it is you have to do or need to be done.

It's the manner in which you ask and when or where you ask that can often get you into trouble. If you're not sure what you're being told to do, you need to politely ask for guidance and direction. If you're presenting a plan to others, make yourself available to explain and provide guidance so they may better understand what needs to be done, with what resources, and to what level they will be judged to have been successful.

Tasks, Conditions, and Standards Example: Parking for the VIP Tour

Ralph got brief instructions from the Center Director about how to reserve parking for the VIP tour. He broke them down into Tasks, Conditions, and Standards to review:

- **Task:** Reserve parking for the VIP tour.
- **Conditions:** During daytime conditions, use parking lot two.
- **Standards:** Make sure there's enough parking for the tour's attendees.

Would that be enough information to be successful in setting up the parking lot? Ralph didn't think so, but he knows the Center Director is really busy, so he asked her to recommend someone he could ask for more guidance. Another team member, who has reserved parking before, was able to give him some advice. He also talked to the parking attendant who works Wednesdays to verify he wasn't missing any details.

Ralph asked more clarity, while being conscientious of the Center Director's time constraints, and wrote down his plan – which he realized could also work as a job aid for team members to use in the future.

Ralph's Tasks, Conditions, and Standards

Task: Set up the parking lot for the VIP tour

- » Communicate with other offices in the building to let them know we will need to reserve spaces, including the day, time, and number of spaces needed.
- » Locate the orange traffic cones to block off spaces.
- » Print a notice for each cone that reads: "This space is reserved for tour attendees at the learning center from 5pm-9pm on [DATE]."
- » Attach the notice to each cone, and place the cones at the head of the parking spaces by 8am.
- » At 3pm, check the spaces that should be reserved. If any are empty, move the cone to the end of the space so no one can park there. Check again at 4pm and 5pm, until all spaces are blocked. This will allow employees on morning shifts to park closer to the building and move their vehicles if needed later in the day.

Conditions: During daytime conditions, use parking lot two

- » Since the VIP tour will be held after closing, we will need to use parking lot one. This means VIPs will be able to park closer to the entrance and not need to walk as far in the dark.
- » The forecast from earlier this week says Wednesday should be a clear evening, but we will double check Wednesday morning. We have umbrellas if it does rain. It's important to know if a significant weather event could occur.

Ralph's Tasks, Conditions, and Standards

Standards: Make sure there's enough parking for the tour

» The morning of the tour, check the number of confirmed tour attendees to ensure there are enough parking spaces reserved for at least one space per attendee. This will ensure there are enough spaces, even if a group or family needs to arrive separately.

Your Turn

Breaking Down These Techniques

Now that we're all familiar with the different techniques, you may have noticed many of them follow a simple pattern:

- » Gather information and resources
- » Make a plan (and maybe a few backup plans)
- » Validate the plan(s)
- » Act on the plan
- » Review/evaluate how the plan went

This is a basic planning cycle, so it makes sense that all our techniques apply the sequence in some way. Hopefully it will become like second nature as you use the techniques more.

Let me just repeat this though: planning is a cycle. Working toward your goals, building better habits, and generally getting to where you want to be is not always going to be a simple, straight path. You'll need to continually check in with yourself: How is this going? Can I do anything to make this process easier or better?

The good thing is that means you don't always have to have the plan 100% perfect the first time around, because you know there will be opportunities to review, evaluate, and modify.

Technique	Primary Goal/Usage	Time to Complete
Range Card	Use a Range Card to evaluate situations, remain true to yourself and your values, and plan next steps by visualizing where you are.	10-15 minutes
PVC-E	PVC-E can be used as a short-term planning objective to support a long-term goal. It allows you to do a quick assessment of where you are in relationship to your personal or professional competition.	15-20 minutes
OODA	OODA is a quick snapshot of a planning process. If you've made a plan using the OODA Loop, you can always revise and go deeper with another technique later.	10-15 minutes
OCOKA	OCOKA allows you to plot a path forward by looking at routes and terrain, obstacles and how to address them, as well as areas of advantage.	20 minutes

Technique	Primary Goal/Usage	Time to Complete
PACE Planning	PACE is a Course of Action planning model – so if you know you'll need a backup plan or two, this technique will help.	15 minutes to a few days, depending on the depth, detail, and size of a goal
METT-TCP	METT-TCP helps you gain a deeper understanding of a goal, how success will be defined, and any holistic considerations needed – like how your actions may be viewed by others or how those close to you might be indirectly affected as you work toward the objective.	10-15 minutes
Tasks, Conditions, and Standards	Tasks, Conditions, and Standards is a quick technique to check a plan and understand what's needed. This technique is helpful for communicating an operation to others.	5-10 minutes

Your Turn

What If These Techniques Don't Work?

A good question, which deserves an honest answer. If something doesn't work, you must ask yourself why. Is it a lack of necessary resources? Lack of understanding what was expected of you? Were you faced with challenges or difficulties, or was there a bump in the planning cycle that caused you to change the plan?

I generally tend to believe when things aren't going well, it's an operator issue. Perhaps I'm cynical, but experience has taught me that the operator is the key functional component in any plan, process, or experience. Ignoring what might have gone wrong or blaming others will only bring you more disappointment.

Just remember that even if you've failed at something, *you aren't a failure*. It's an important distinction. Many people have given up goals under the weight of that painful label, but who you are is defined by so many more things than something that didn't work out. When you realize failure is an action – something you did rather than who you are – it's a lot easier to see what went wrong and grow from it.

Failure is an integral part of being successful. If you approach it as an opportunity to evaluate yourself and your ability to plan and follow through, then you will do better. Be honest – if something is not right, take the needed steps to repair the situation. Trust me on this.

Do you feel a sense of accomplishment when you're part of a success? Of course! Analyzing success is easy; analyzing a failure takes courage and honesty. In evaluating what went wrong, you just might find a communication problem existed or a simple tweak to a process is needed. Or you may discover the entire process, though it looked good on paper, could not have been successfully implemented when reality struck. Failures and disappointments allow us opportunities to gain success.

Many years ago, I was in charge of moving some materials through a building. It seemed easy:

- » Bring items from point A to point B.
- » Don't lose anything, and don't break anything.
- » Have it done within one hour so as not to disrupt the operations of the building.

Too easy – at least on paper – but in reality, not so much. We were missing details, so my team and I started to ask questions to fill in the blanks. To do this, we visited the buffet of techniques I mentioned earlier. We needed to identify check points, obstacles, left and right peripherals, the standard of what success would look like, etc.

As I listed some of the points to clarify, the team and I started to pencil them in on our Range Card. Can you think of any additional questions, details, or items we could have added to our list?

- » When did this task need to be completed? Was there a target completion date/time?
- » How big were these items?
- » Would point B be ready to receive the items when we arrived?
- » What was the safest route to take? Was the safest route also the quickest?
- » How long would it ideally take to move the materials?
- » How would we move the items? Would we need carts, a hand dolly, or would we simply carry them?
- » What exactly did "so as not to disrupt the operations of the building" really mean?
- » How did the route we were going to travel look? Would any building maintenance be going on?

As we explored exactly what needed to be accomplished, we were able to put our plan down on paper. We identified the goal/objective, picked our primary and alternate routes, walked the terrain to check safety and efficiency, identified stakeholders, communicated our plan, asked for feedback, and got our plan approved. The movement went well, safely, and on time. The team received high marks.

It does seem like we had a lot of questions for such a simple task, but by working together, the Troops knew the plan, were comfortable with the plan, knew the route to be taken, understood all the potential impacts (Conditions), and they knew what had to be done to accomplish the goal (Standards).

If only everything had gone smoothly.

What is the last part of all our planning? To look back, review, and evaluate. Sure, we got great marks, and we were happy with our efforts, but could we have done anything differently? Did we miss anything?

Believe it or not, we found a few, small considerations that might have helped us. Remember how we weren't supposed "to disrupt the operations of the building"? Well, in the grand scheme of things, we didn't disrupt the operations of the *entire* building... but one of the employees did ask, "Why didn't you wait until the end of business, when most employees had gone home, and the route would have been less traveled?"

Lesson learned for the next time!

 Remember: Failure is an integral part of being successful. Analyzing success is easy; analyzing a failure takes courage and honesty.

Sometimes – and I know I've done this – we try to do too much and don't have the experience, knowledge, or resources to accomplish a task. Just remember that every big task is a sequence of smaller, less complicated steps. Each small success builds on the one before, growing until you reach your goal.

If any of these techniques have not worked for you, try breaking down the task you've laid out into smaller, more manageable pieces. I always start with the easiest of steps. I ask myself, "What do I need to accomplish today?" Laundry, call my mom (Hi mom!), go to the store, vacuum, work on a project, etc. As the list grows and becomes more detailed, I have to ask myself: What tasks are a priority? What could be done later? What can be done at the same time? Thus, the plan begins to naturally take shape.

Don't worry if things don't click right away. Management is a process, but life is a journey. Enjoy the challenges and the views.

Conclusion

What does all of this mean? It means nothing if we don't learn from it, or if we can't be honest with ourselves and in our interactions with others.

Where did you want to be today? Where do you want to be tomorrow? In a month, a year, five years? Really, openly and with honesty, ask yourself – not about where someone else wants you to be or where you want them to be – but about where you want to be, now or more than five years from now. What are your goals, aspirations, dreams, and needs?

Life is about learning from our past experiences and watching others. We can learn from the things we screwed up and from what others have screwed up. (That might explain why I love people-watching at the airport.) The same goes for learning from ours and others' successes.

How can you achieve success? By planning, anticipating, being flexible, having an alternate plan, maintaining your focus, and being positive about yourself and your ability to be successful in your efforts.

Resources

Suggested Reading

U.S. Army Ranger Handbook by the U.S. Department of Defense

How to Stop Worrying and Start Living by Dale Carnegie

How to Win Friends and Influence People by Dale Carnegie

Jonathan Livingston Seagull by Richard Bach

Glossary

Act: the first step in putting a plan into action. *Used in OODA.*

Alternate Plan: developed alongside the Primary Plan (PP) to support it if anything goes wrong; remains fairly close to the PP, and with only some minor variation. *Used in PACE Planning.*

Alternative Route: similar to the Primary Route and still a good option, but it might have more obstacles or take longer. *Used in OCOKA.*

Avenues of Approach: how you move along a chosen route based on the terrain. This could be planning guidelines or the mindset you adopt. *Used in OCOKA.*

Civilians (On The Battlefield) (COTB): people in your life who may not be directly involved with a goal but who will influence and/or be affected by your pursuit of it. *Used in: METT-TCP.*

Competition: anything that could be competing for your time or focus while pursuing a goal. *Used in: PVC-E.*

Resources

Concealment: something that allows you to observe what's happening around you while obscuring your position. *Used in OCOKA.*

Conditions: constraints to operate under. These could be the resources you will have or need. *Used in Tasks, Conditions, and Standards.*

Contingency Plan: a plan that's very different from the Primary or Alternative Plan, but that still supports the overall goal. *Used in PACE Planning.*

Contingency Route: a route that will get you there but is the least desirable path. *Used in OCOKA.*

Course of Action (CoA): a plan that covers the purpose or intent of a goal, the strategies and actions that will be used to accomplish it, and any expected conditions or requirements. A CoA should be suitable, feasible, acceptable, distinguishable, and complete. *Used in OODA.*

Cover: provides protection and hides you from the enemy. *Used in OCOKA.*

Date Time Group (DTG): the date and time an assessment or plan is made. *Used in Range Card.*

Decide: point in OODA planning where you create a Course of Action (CoA). *Used in OODA.*

Dead Space: areas you cannot readily see but know something is there. *Used in Range Card.*

Equipment: resources are needed to complete a task. *Used in METT-TCP.*

Evaluation: an honest review that takes a set of tasks, placed against a measure of success, and determines if the measures of success were achieved. *Used in PVC-E.*

Final Protective Line (FPL): the farthest you can go before straying into someone else's space or betraying one of your own personal boundaries. *Used in Range Card.*

Key Terrain: areas that could give an advantage. For example, you should choose the best time/place to present an idea or give feedback. *Used in OCOKA, METT-TCP.*

Known Distance Markers: objects ahead that you already know the distance to from your current position. *Used in Range Card.*

Left and Right Limits: imaginary lines identifying your area of responsibility, stretching from your location to a designated point. *Used in Range Card.*

Magnetic North: what is leading you forward and providing direction. *Used in: Range Card.*

Mission: the goal you're trying to accomplish. *Used in METT-TCP.*

Non-Commissioned Officers (NCOs): Non-commissioned officers usually earn positions of authority by promotion through the enlisted ranks. A commissioned officer is an officer who has rank before officially assuming their role, usually because they enter the military after receiving a post-secondary degree.

Observe/Observation: taking in your surroundings and being situationally aware, allowing you to plot a path forward. *Used in OODA, OCOKA.*

Obstacles: issues, roadblocks, or weaknesses we can observe in a specific area. *Used in: Range Card, OCOKA.*

Orient: adjusting actions and resources toward what you need to do. *Used in OODA.*

Resources

Peripheral Vision: similar to Left/Right Limits, peripheral vision looks at what is around you and how you tie into the person/position on your left and right. *Used in PVC-E.*

Political Considerations: how your actions, results, and capabilities will be viewed by others. *Used in METT-TCP.*

Primary Plan: the best plan, which will use the best methodology and thus give the best results. *Used in PACE Planning.*

Primary Route: the best route, which will best support your movement toward the objective. *Used in OCOKA.*

Standards: specifications or variables used to define success. *Used in Tasks, Conditions, and Standards.*

Target Reference Points (TRP): easily recognizable, always visible locations (natural or manmade) used for target acquisition and to determine range. *Used in Range Card.*

Tasks: exactly what needs to be done; the objective, goal, and any related or dependent duties. *Used in Tasks, Conditions, and Standards.*

Terrain: See key terrain.

Time Available: how much time you have to complete a task or goal. *Used in METT-TCP.*

Troops: the people supporting or working on a goal together. *Used in METT-TCP.*

Acknowledgements

There are many people I need to thank for where I am and who I am. I've learned from some highly educated people, and I've learned from many people who may not have had a lot of formal education – but they had interesting and valuable life experiences that taught them a great many things, and I was fortunate they shared their experiences with me.

To the dedicated teachers I had at Salesian High School, thank you for having the patience to look at a confused and awkward young man and tell him you believed in him (even if he didn't believe in himself). FR. Frank SBD, Flash, Mr. Toolan, Mr. Donavan, Bro.'s Jim, Bert and Bob, and all of the other teachers I passed in the hallways... Thank you so much. Your wisdom and guidance has served me well.

I'd like to thank the Non-Commissioned Officers who saw something in me that I didn't see or believe was inside me. They taught me that a leader leads from the front; never ask your soldiers to do anything you weren't willing to first do yourself; make sure your people know what's going on; and there will be times you'll have to make the hard, unpopular – but right – choice over the easy and popular wrong. There are just too many of these fine NCOs to name and list, but I'm sure they know who they are.

I'd also like to thank the officers I served with who understood that NCOs make things happen, and good NCOs make good things happen. Thank you for the opportunity to work with you, learn from you, and for giving me opportunities to excel.

I need to thank my children D&D; they inspire me to do better and make them proud of me, and without them, I would have never been able to accomplish many of the things I've done, and still want to do. I will never be able to express the pride and love I have when I think of you. You've saved

Acknowledgements

me from myself on more than one occasion and in more ways than you'll ever know. Thank you for all the laughter, tears, giggles, hugs, and smiles!

To my family and friends, I don't believe I can ever say thank you enough. Without your belief in me, support, and encouragement, I wouldn't be here. You've all stood with me through many difficult times. Thank you. I need to give a special thanks to Steve and Noel. You pulled me up when I needed to be reminded how important family and friends are. Thank you so very much.

I'd like to thank you, reader, for getting this book. The fact you're reading it fulfills one of my life goals, and it tells me you wanted to learn some management techniques for your life just like me. Thank you for your support and belief in this book. I hope your journey is as exciting and fulfilling as mine has been for me. Always believe in yourself and your ability to achieve great things. Don't waiver in believing in who you are and your capacity to learn, love, and live!

I need to thank my higher power for keeping me grounded, allowing me to learn from my mistakes, and to know that even when all seems lost, it never is – I just need to ask for help and guidance.

I have to take a moment to thank my parents. Mom, Dad – thank you, thank you, thank you. I know I wasn't always where you wanted or expected me to be in life, and I know there was many a night where sleep did not come easy as you worried about me, what I was doing, and how I was doing. Though it must have been difficult at times, I know you never wavered in your love for me and your belief in who I was and who I was going to be. Thank you, thank you, and thank you again.

Thank you all for believing in me and believing in my journey.

John

About the Author

John Riotte has traveled the world, jumped out of planes, and generally learned how to plan for events and for life. After serving in the military for 20 years, he changed careers, moving into radio for a short time; then to security, training, and instructing others in higher level security; working for the DOD, DOE, and finally as a Global Security Data Center Area Security Manager.

John is the proud father of Danielle and Andrew, as well as the (very) proud Pop-Pop to his granddaughter Bobbi.